GREEN ANIMALS ON THE PLANET

Speedy Publishing LLC
40 E. Main St. #1156
Newark, DE 19711
www.speedypublishing.com

Animals produce colour in different ways. There are several separate reasons why animals have evolved colours. Camouflage enables an animal to remain hidden from view. Signalling enables an animal to communicate information such as warning of its ability to defend itself.

AFRICAN BULLFROG

is a large frog, with males weighing 1.4 kg, females are half the size, making it unique among frogs, as in most amphibians females are usually larger than males. African bullfrog is carnivorous and a voracious eater, eating insects, small rodents, reptiles, small birds and other amphibians.

FIGEATER BEETLE

is a member of the scarab beetle family. Figeaters are very docile and don't bite humans. Their ability to only eat soft and overripe fruit means they aren't damaging to gardens since they are limited to only eating fruit that has already fallen or been pecked open by birds.

GREEN TREE PYTHON

is characterized by a relatively slim body. The species usually reaches a total length of 4.9-5.9 ft, but large females may reach 6.6 ft. They are found in Indonesia, Florida U.S.A., Papua New Guinea and Australia. Its main habitat is typically in or near rainforest, residing in trees, shrubs and bushes.

GILDED HUMMINGBIRD

is found in lightly wooded country, including parks and gardens, over central-southern South America, from northeast Bolivia south to Uruguay and northern Argentina. It is overall greenish-golden with a coppery tail, whitish-buff underparts, a rufous chin, and a slightly decurved, black-tipped red bill.

CHAMELEON

are found in warm habitats that range from rain forest to desert conditions. Chameleons vary greatly in size and body structure, with maximum total lengths varying from 15 mm to 68.5 cm. Chameleons have the most distinctive eyes of any reptile. Each eye can pivot and focus independently, allowing the chameleon to observe two different objects simultaneously.

GREEN MORAY EEL

These eels average 1.8 in length, but can grow up to 2.5 m long and weigh up to 29 kg. They are often camouflaged to hide in the reef from unsuspecting prey. Green morays are nocturnal predators with poor eyesight that primarily use their sense of smell to hunt.

GREEN LYNX SPIDER

is a very bright green spider, about 19 mm in length, with long, spiny legs and an oblong to oval abdomen. This spider is found in southern United States from coast to coast, and also in Mexico and Central America. It often lives in clumps of prickly pear cactus.

WHITE-LIPPED PIT VIPER

is nocturnal, and when aroused is quick to bite though this is seldom fatal. The white-lipped pit viper can be found in forest, shrubland, plains, agricultural areas, and gardens. Usually found off the ground in trees or bushes.

EMERALD SWALLOWTAIL

is native to southeast
Asia, but regularly kept
in butterfly zoos around
the world. Emerald
Swallowtail has a
wingspan reaching about
8–10 centimetres. This
species gets its name from
the bright emerald green
band that runs across
each of its dark greenish-
black wings.

GREEN SEA URCHIN

is commonly found
in northern waters
all around the world
including both the Pacific
and Atlantic Oceans. The
green sea urchin prefers
to eat seaweeds but will
eat other organisms. Sea
urchins are dioecious,
meaning they either
contain male or female
reproductive organs.

GREEN IGUANA

is a large, arboreal, mostly herbivorous species of lizard. Iguana can fall up to 50 feet and land unhurt. During cold, wet weather, green iguanas prefer to stay on the ground for greater warmth. The native range of the green iguana extends from southern Mexico to central Brazil, Dominican Republic, Paraguay, and Bolivia and the Caribbean.

PLAIN PARAKEET

is endemic to Brazil. Their natural habitats include open country with trees and bushes, lowland evergreen forest areas, second-growth forests, degraded former forest areas, partially cultivated land, woodlands, parks and urban areas. The plain parakeet is noticeable for being plain green all over.

RED-EYED TREE FROG

is not poisonous and rely
on camouflage to protect
themselves. Red-eyed
tree frogs are insectivores
that eat crickets, moths,
flies, and other insects.
Being green helps the red-
eyed tree frog blend in
with tree leaves.

PRAYING MANTIS

is named for its prominent
front legs, which are
bent and held together
at an angle that suggests
the position of prayer.
Praying mantis are highly
predacious and feed
on a variety of insects,
including moths, crickets,
grasshoppers and flies.
Praying mantis are often
protectively colored to
the plants they live on.